Claudio Ottaviano

THE SEA

AND OTHER BULLSHIT

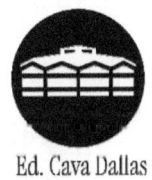

Ed. Cava Dallas

Dedicated to Stefani Germanotta a.k.a. Lady Gaga

Second edition, revised and uncensored.

Collection The Great Poetry of the Twentieth Century.

Printed in 1969. All rights reserved.

Copyright © 2024 Claudio Ottaviano.

WWW.CLAUDIOOTTAVIANO.COM

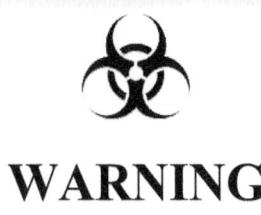

WARNING

The poems contained in this book may include language or content that some people may find offensive and/or disturbing.

DISCLAIMER

Any reference to real people, facts, or events in this work is purely coincidental and unintentional. Any resemblance to real persons or actual events is purely coincidental. This book is protected by copyright. Unauthorized reproductions, modifications, distributions, or sales are prohibited. The poems contained in this book are works of fiction and should not be considered as descriptions of real events or as reflections of the author's opinions or beliefs. The author and the publisher assume no responsibility for any direct or indirect, material or immaterial damages arising from the use or reliance on the poems contained in this book. The purchase or reading of this book does not create any professional relationship between the author or publisher and the reader. No animals were harmed in the making of this book. This book is intended for an adult audience and may contain content or themes that may not be suitable for younger readers. Reader discretion is advised. The author assumes no responsibility for the interpretation or effect that the content may have on the reader. Readers are encouraged to consider their own emotional well-being and to stop reading if the content becomes uncomfortable or inappropriate.

PLEASE READ WITH CAUTION

All non-original images contained in this book are used for fair use under Article 70 of the Italian Copyright Law (L.633/1941).

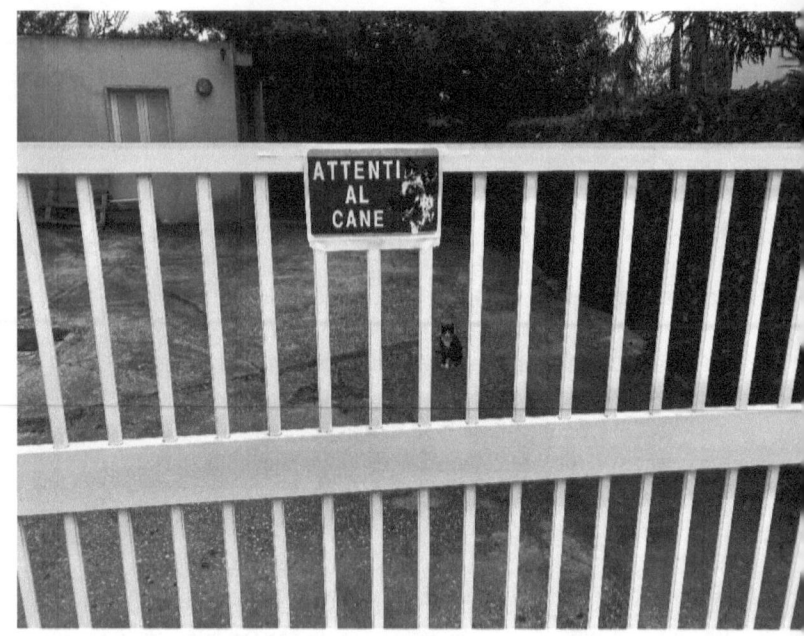

JAZZ AND OTHER PERPLEXITIES
BY Andrea G.G. Parasiliti

Claudio Ottaviano, I don't know if he's a poet but I couldn't care less about that.

All I know is that he's a friend whom I find in my house on my sofa in Playa Grande after many years, when I thought I would never see him again.

Claudio, a man of jazz, a double bassist of drunken Milanese nights at the *Buca di San Vincenzo*, blue nights and dried-up, withered canals, left Milan and the double bass to settle in Sicily, in the solitude of a wolf and an oilman of Cava D'Aliga, all Mediterranean menstrual flows bleeding ink among lost loves.

And yet Claudio sees the horror of a Sicily far from tourist dreams, cinematic and nostalgic, all myths, cassatelle, and sausages, bringing us back to existential questions, perennial, always the same: where do I come from, who am I, where am I going.

Adding the further, never banal, space-time question: what the hell am I doing here?

Forgotten coasts where the dawn is all a grin of dogs, chasing each other among houses inhabited only in summer.

Children playing in the morning, in front of the enchanting sea, making paper boats blown by the wind but no one sends them to school.

Cheap prostitutes more welcoming than the old aunt on Sunday, while the global geopolitical risk reaches you in the black hole darkroom where you hope no one finds you and then you can only say attention my dear sirs, listen to me well...

Because here it's nothing for everything to go to hell.

Playa Grande (Scicli)
18 April 2024
3 am

Andrea G.G. Parasiliti

"The straight road

is a maze."

- Anonymous

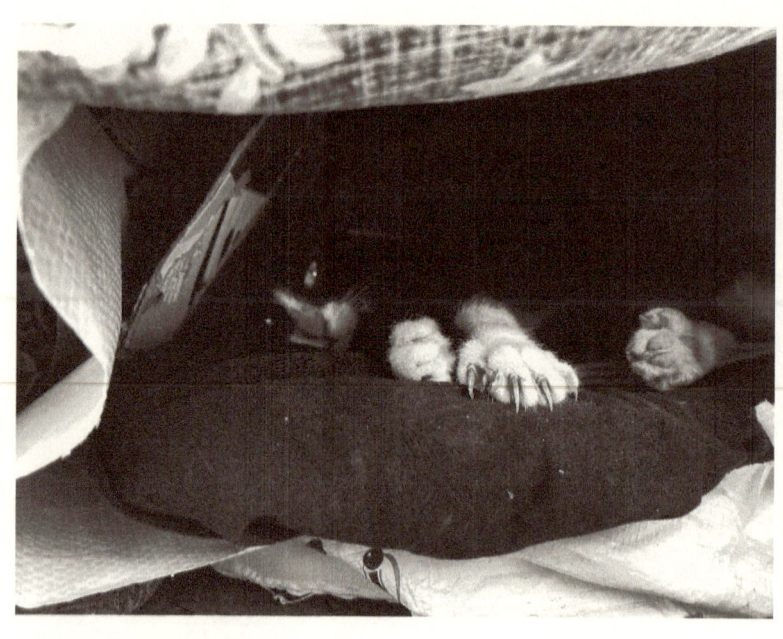

EXOCULATIONS.*

---

* Neologism from the verb "to inoculate", just google it.

At Zeus's passing,

he pierces the eye with a needle

and gathers the worms from the blood,

but he's not a doctor

nor even a shaman,

just Tano, the husband of the daughter

of the lady from the tobacco shop

when you enter Porto Palo.

Last night I dreamed

of a person who was sleeping,

and my life

was his dream.

***

She's out on the terrace,

back turned, long hair

witch-like, reaching

down to her waist.

Behind her, the cliff and

the luminous sea that sparkles

in a hypnotic kaleidoscope

of magical crystals.

Her left hand

rests on

the azure railing

while with her right,

almost in slow motion,

she takes a drag from her cigarette

and blows out the smoke

that begins to swirl

in a chaotic geometry,

like Eros's subconscious.

From the cool shadow

of the room,

lying naked on the bed,

I watch her, enchanted,

following the slow,

sensual movements

of her artist's hands

and her ethereal body

that seems to dance

like a white wedding dress

in a meadow of paradise flowers

when suddenly

"The knife sharpener's here,

knives, scissors, forks."

***

Blood-free gaze

intercepts

things falling

under an obscene sky.

Mercury flowing

in blood through

tuna cans.

Shadow extending

across the iris with a needle.

Black spot

bridge disconnecting

the walls of time.

Glare.

Oh puzzle men

who chew with dogs

who mark walls with lipstick

but above all

who scatter on the streets

the ashes of witches.

Oh puzzle men

hear my words and

be very careful

because here it's nothing

for everything to go to hell.

Abraxas

Beauty at dawn

you wander a little lost

in the first blue

makeup falls to the ground

the night in your heart

does not end

when the rooster

crows cock-a-doodle-doo.

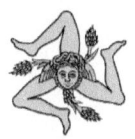

The imaginary and nonexistent Sicily
of intellectuals, travelers, and the Godfather,
doesn't interest us because,
from the Greeks to the Italians,
no one has ever managed to tame the Sicilian.

There's a girl sunbathing topless,
Montalbano-Effect,
in my underwear.

Flocks of seagulls

carry in their beaks

human organs

in a nest of emptiness

they assemble bodies on branches

fly and fly the seagulls.

These old folks with iPads,

grown up in an era where

more concrete, asphalt, and tar flowed,

and the cooler you were,

they understand as much about nature

as a dried fig.

The dog broke

under the child's feet

who cries and barks

out of sadness.

***

In the void,

distant lights

engulfed by the sea

at the mercy of the she-wolf

I watched the oil tanker.

Black and gloomy,

ship full of ghosts

aiming straight

at the center of my thoughts.

Black iron

cutting through the night

while the light began

to flow like

a generous stream

of menstrual blood.

Ah, today I must remember

to make that phone call.

***

Hidden mirrors

People travel

beyond the husks of bodies

they walk through forests

bleeding ink

in the shadow of objects

dreaming of lost loves.

***

DEFRAG.EXE

Beauty corroded by pixels

oceans of acid blood.

Living mercury

erotic attraction

you run in the woods

with the monkeys.

Thunder takes

the shape of a diamond,

bodies burn

on the cliff.

The sad vision of silence

gaze infected by time.

White light

is the underground dawn

the clock

merges with the asphalt.

Iron face

watches you from the future

burns the line

of the horizon.

Defrag.exe

is the dawn of my new flesh,

the monkeys run in the woods.

Defrag.exe

Vision of an eternal tunnel

I had you, I loved you,

I lose you.

***

***

A doll

inside Angela's room

unsettles me.

Angela doesn't live here anymore.

Her uninhabited room

is ruled by the doll.

I can barely refrain

from wrapping the doll

with adhesive tape

to suffocate it.

But it's so cute...

Thanks to a mechanism
standing up it has open eyes
and lying down instead
it has closed eyes.

It seems alive,
but it's dead instead.

***

Anemic gaze

hidden by the earth

a repository of memories

and clipped nails,

the scent of the faint body

weaves

among the white sheets.

***

Let's go to the beach

Families

like the penguins

in documentaries,

dad yelling

at his son to get out

of the sea because

he has to go eat spaghetti,

teenagers hiding

to smoke a few cigarettes,

in short, a beach

like many others.

But my attention is captured

by two old folks, perhaps over 90,

holding hands

walking slow and unsure.

A bit further, a 16-year-old

pimply with messy hair

follows their movement

capturing it with

an old camcorder.

The curly-haired kid captures the entire silent

walk of the elderly couple

and perhaps he too senses

that it was their

last laborious walk

on the beach of Cava D'Aliga.

***

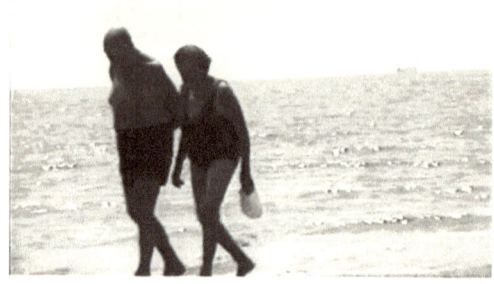

*WORK FAST - WORK CHEAP**

This book

in my mind

was a great book,

grandiose in its formless cloud

of expectations and dark patterns,

it was the perfect poetry book,

I wanted to be eloquent.

But line after line,

the ideal slipped into reality,

taking shape and colliding

with the frustration of the real.

Work is a squalid trauma.

Famous motto attributed to Brian Eno. I also recommend checking out his "Oblique Strategies".

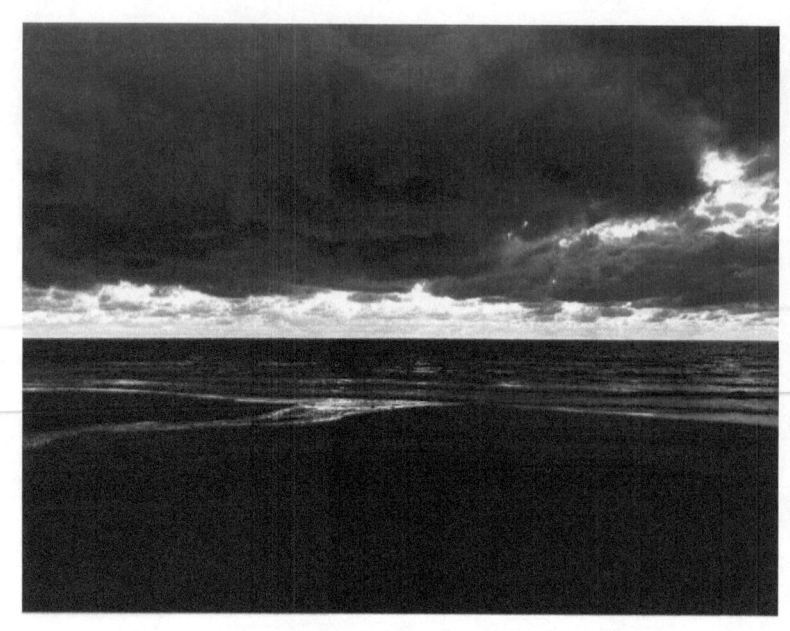

HORIZON

The seagull

is a cage.

I wrote to you,

come see the stars

on the terrace.

While waiting under the stars

I rolled a joint.

I waited for you and

at one point I hear

noise on the stairs.

Adrenaline rush

but it wasn't you,

it was just a cat.

I waited for you

but you didn't come.

Blurred blade

that cuts and separates

bodies from time.

Infinite trauma

behind the sea.

Love embraces us

overlaps our boundaries

spreads to the horizon

a common skin

we will be inseparable

despite the abyss.

Recorder

The painter makes a mark on the canvas:

    it remains.

The writer writes a word:

    it remains.

The musician plays a note:

    it disappears.

The Search for Happiness

I reach out my hand

fraying my soul

I stretch

ever thinner

disappearing into a thread.

***

Santa Cruz

Crusader of the sick tribe,

astronaut dead

in space.

A warrior defends

the door of light

while the fridge

chirps like crickets.

Unperturbed, we're watched

by the faces of ancestors from the future,

masks of serious iron

of lunar coolness.

The door of light opens

unknown designs on the horizon.

You can feel the strength

of the other warriors,

an army of skeletons

we're not alone

we've entered a level.

We are a sun.

***

The surface of love

cuts away the skin

from the bodies written

scratched

filled with ink,

it reaches the pure body

dripping

red,

organs exposed

in an embrace

container

of alien thought.

Sue me Sciascia!

Talking about the province
is the least provincial thing
you can do in the province.

From a window onto emptiness

the body leans towards collapse

eroded by the sea

it turns into sand.

The rocks are thoughts

desperate under a rain

of magnetic fragments

striving to fill the sky.

Almost friends

The news came out

in the Ragusa newspaper

that my cousin Giovanni

who lives in London

played basketball at the court

with the actor Adam Sandler.

Out of the 20 people in the photo,

Adam doesn't know who Giovanni is.

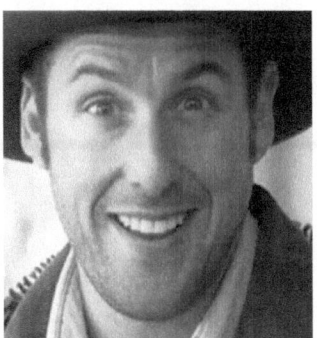

Aperol

Elegantly naked

she breathes in the pink sunset

and then vomits the spritz.

The dam implodes

horizon blurred

eaten by the sky and the sea,

deity victim

of its own magic,

and meanwhile in the eye

of the catastrophe

an unsettling calm

foresees no future.

Not in the moods of time

not among the thorns of memories

the shape of the house

is written in the stars.

Hmm, interesting.

Who smokes a cigar
accompanies it with a prestigious whiskey
sitting next to the lit fireplace
leafing through a good book
(not this one you have in your hands).

But not him:
Freud accompanied his cigar
with reclining people who
talked about their affairs.

He smoked
to give shape to the spirit,
to manage the spark
to avoid speaking.

***

Only light

a non-color

that the brain

calls white.

Cosmic union

with the spirits

of people

you have known

and forgotten.

It gives you nirvana

a creamy vanilla wind,

the color of the paper

of this book,

but just a little more yellow.

But a breath,

lizard tail

that wriggles,

nervous drops

of mad mercury.

A spark

and the fire flares up.

Answer that final call.

Then we close the bar. Rise to the surface.

One breath

and you'll no longer

be afraid of anything.

***

Snow-crash

Footprints in the silence

of pixelated bodies

walk along the edges

of snowy screens.

I was reading Tex on the plane

I needed to pee

since I had left

home for the airport.

Just when

I unfasten my seatbelt

to get up from my seat

"We inform the kind passengers

that we are approaching

a region of significant turbulence,

please keep your seat belts fastened

remain seated blablabla..."

DING!

The little bathroom sign is red.

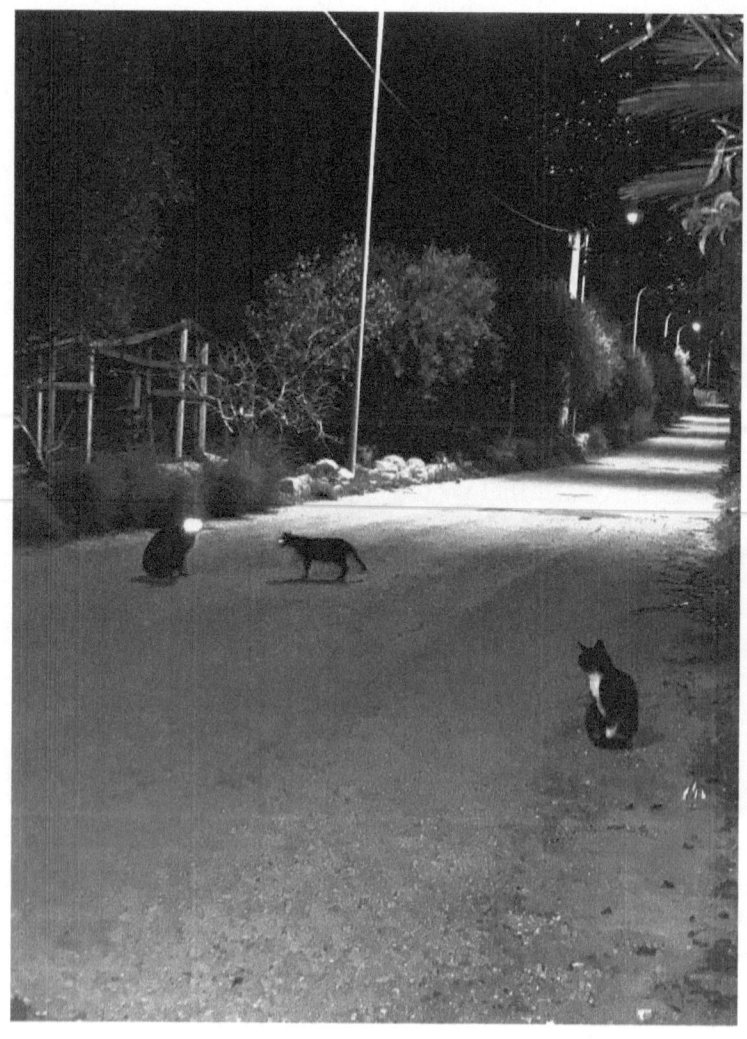

NOCTURNAL ANIMALS

Confidences of an Eccentric

There's a castle in France

where once every 9 years

the most terrible

game of chance is played:

the game of goose.

To be invited

to those tables with 7 seats

is the true zenith of the gambler.

The suicide rate

in the year following the tournament

is currently 37.2%.

It's not a joke.

***

In a room

in a hotel by the highway.

On the white sheets
a splatter of alien blood.

Options:
1 - menstrual blood
2 - a junkie has overdosed
3 - stabbing

The heating doesn't work
but too much paranoia
to call the front desk
or rather he didn't know
what number to dial
so he improvises like Parker
unrolling toilet paper and

starting a small fire

in the shower.

He watches the traffic

waiting for a miracle.

***

It doesn't make sense

It doesn't make sense
to pay 100 euros for an aperitif.
It doesn't make sense
to take 2 hours from Acitrezza to Catania.
It doesn't make sense to hit
a pothole and blow a tire.
It doesn't make sense to drive
to Cava Dallas at 20 km/h
with a blown tire.
It doesn't make sense
to find yourself without the money
to change the tire.
It doesn't make sense
to stay angry in the little town
writing poems
that don't make sense.

Paper scraps and waste

that slither

along the street

like snakes

animated by the wind.

A man kicks

an empty pot

rolling on the sidewalk.

Our words

are cats

meowing

among the ruins.

You're not selling me a guitar
You're not selling me a keyboard
or a new revolutionary plug-in,
you're selling me
the dream of being a professional,
when being a professional
is a nightmare.

Cockroaches are just dates with legs.

***

Finanze Street

None of the classmates
from the 3rd section of Parini school
believed he would really go through with it:
they already had their smirk ready
and were gossiping about him.

From the dark walls of the street
like visions, materialized
women in black and white
offered themselves
like sirens on the cliffs.
Some smiled tenderly,
some untouchable and ethereal
like a statue made of steam

turned their gaze elsewhere.

Violently, a door opened
and a hand threw
a basin of water into the street:
what a scare, but he kept walking
and the little companions,
a bunch
of liliputian skeletons,
followed the naive
and frivolous leader.

Behind a shutter
an ancient voice calls out
"my dear boy, come here,
I'll make your milk go out".

Meanwhile, a sweet big black dog
suddenly found himself grazing

in the middle of the street

for a moment

time stood still

and everyone admired him.

From afar

a speeding car,

seeing the dog,

accelerates even more.

The dog, overwhelmed,

whines for half an hour.

***

Among flowers and snails

in a pond of blood

play the hopping frogs.

The ticking of a clock

flows from the white nest of spiders

while fire butterflies

fly and write

with charcoal on a mirror.

But did you put rape drugs

in my beer?

***

Robert De Lirio

(Named so

because during a musical entertainment

at a wedding

he locked himself in the bathroom with the bride).

Still sweaty from the concert

sadly dazed

he walked down the corridor

of that anonymous hotel

towards room 119,

as the key said.

A vague premonition

of the early morning pickup

that would await him the next morning

hovered in his mind, making him perspire

a slight formal discomfort

through that wall of alcohol

and drugs that anesthetized him

giving him temporary relief.

At the level of room 115

Robert stops walking

and stands in the middle

of the empty corridor.

He hears the sensual moans and breaths of a female

Ahhhh, ahhhhh, ahhh.

Those moans both excite him

and unsettle him at the same time.

There is no one

as he doubts himself

and in the middle of the corridor

he jerks off...

...since it's deep into the night.

In the morning Robert

after sticking two fingers

down his throat, taking a shit, and showering

goes down to the lobby

for breakfast.

"Robert last night

on *Heart Of Glass* you missed

the modulation of the last

chorus! And throughout the concert

you were rushing the tempo!":

Breakfast

with the band colleagues

was as usual.

Robert notices

behind Pino (the guitarist)
a certain commotion:
The concierge bustling around
a certain coming and going and
finally an ambulance arrives.

Robert quickly asks a waiter
what was happening:
"Unfortunately, a lady,
one of our elderly guests this morning
was found lifeless
in her room.
Unfortunately, these things happen
we apologize for the inconvenience".

***

NISNIR

It's time to quit Prince Of Persia

otherwise chaos will ensue

or perhaps it has already begun.

Drunk Viscid stares at me

with his little whore

tasting like musky rose

fresh from a trip to Interland.

Among enchanted yellow books

and testaments of impossible suicides

there's a white man

his name is Nick Gerr

also known as Viscid.

But the mosquito I killed last night

was just a mosquito

or was it the metamorphosis of a prostitute?

***

Milano, August 2001

When the streetlights dim
and the ghosts evaporate
from the asphalt, the footsteps
of someone are melodies
that fall into emptiness
and the few cars
are solitary waves.

The night is made
for grazing.

I find myself walking
until dawn, aimlessly,
and when the city
starts to stir

I take a photo

with the automatic camera

at Porta Genova.

The night is a black hole,

a darkroom to develop

images.

***

***

Roma Square

The boys were out of their minds,

the right substance was coursing through them.

Giovanni tossed up

a cassette tape,

and rolled up the monument.

Some played in the fountain,

some rolled on the grass,

others tried

to tear apart a bench.

A pack of animals.

Riccardo, calm with his guitar

under those long blond hair
full of Valium
tried to play
some Nirvana songs
singing in his watered-down
English.

Samir supplied the group
his arms full of cuts
each cut was a day in jail
and he had the refined habit
of spitting on his tattoo
before every sip of beer.
A magical ritual,
he said.

Friends, the city, the night
were waiting for me with open arms,
always ready for a reality check

with the naive claim

of knowing the world by challenging it.

Among the boys of the pack,

stretching out on the sidewalks of Via Etnea,

there was also Marco Uau, proudly wearing

a pair of shoes he had

stolen from a Falco,

the special police in Catania.

You could hear Marco Uau coming

from kilometers away, indeed he shouted

Ua-ua-uuuuaaaauauuuuuuuuuuuuuuuuuuuuuuuuuu.

He ended up arrested for

cutting the heads off a couple of swans

from the pond in Villa Bellini.

Samir also ended up in jail.

Riccardo, on the other hand, died of an overdose,

there on the ground, in Piazza Roma,

with his cheap guitar in his arms.

***

***

Mimmo 11 Settembre

Every Thursday evening,

the Bamboccioni Swing Band

performed at the Toilet Club,

a dump with floors

sticky with alcohol and vomit.

"Elegant 1940s swing quartet"

so said the poster.

Instead of chairs,

there were

ceramic toilets in the venue.

While the quartet played,

two burlesque dancers,

after sniffing

even the plaster in the dressing rooms,

animated the empty dance floor.

Mimmo 11 September,

named for the bombs

he dropped on the drums,

played while staring

at the dancers' asses and tits.

Sometimes he had blackouts,

missed the cues,

forgot which song

they were playing, and

according to some,

even forgot

himself.

After the show,

the Bamboccioni Swing Band

took their pay,

30 measly euros under the table

(A few damn bucks but immediate),

and went to the Diesel nightclub

where on Thursday nights

the legendary Pervert night took place.

Mimmo 11 September

in his alcohol-fueled dances

hooks up with a stunning blonde girl

and dances with her

passionately.

His bandmates

approach him

and warn him,

"that's a dude."

Mimmo bursts out laughing
and thinks it's a joke.
There was no way he was
swaying
over a transvestite.

***

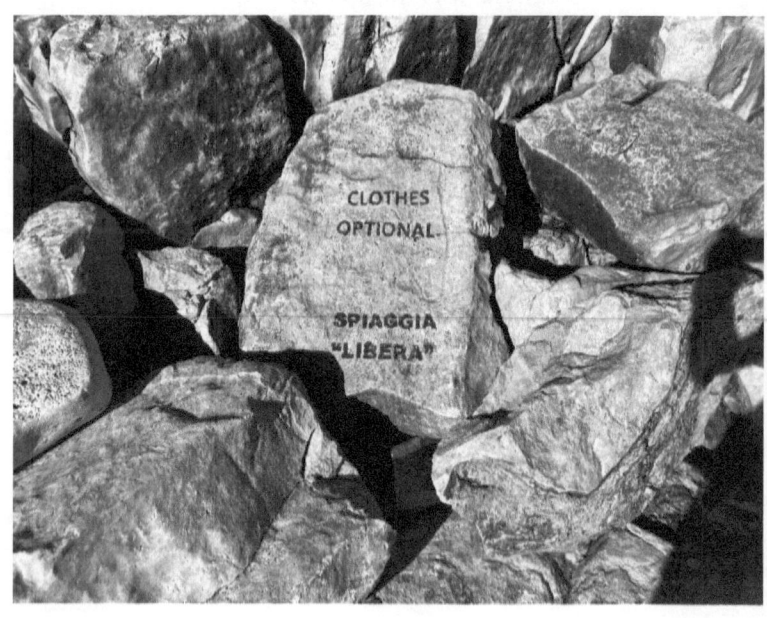

THE SIRENS

The sirens were omniscient.

You _____ are not. You are ignorant.

Did you know that the sirens

didn't have fish tails

but rather feathered bird wings?

Did you know they perched on the cliffs

at the volatile boundary between sky and earth?

Did you know that the word "siren"

means both singing and cord

and that the English word "*string*" comes from there?

Did you know that in the Middle Ages

the word becomes *strega* (witch)

meaning she who binds?

Fur Elise

Na-na-na-na-na

Na-na-na-na.

***

The Two Sicilies

A bored shrug on the phone
in the realm of contradiction
where animate and inanimate
meet and blur
balancing between dominant cultures
and obscure, private cults.

Watching the sun
while sipping a cappuccino
between reason and magic
is intellectual perversion,
a wild whirlpool of
many masks
but few faces.

A savvy shopping trip to Eurospin
with working formulas
interactions like puppets.

Sicily has a heart of a chasm
if you dig, you find skulls
but at the checkout
there's the friendly cashier.

***

Tell me about yourself, beautiful Siren,

tell me about yourself

for I am not afraid

if I feel like

vomiting ink.

I'm used to it.

It walks on the tongue

before the sound

after the voice

it gives itself to the vault.

Damn, I'm exhausted.

We digital Ulysses of the sea
bound to the totem hate the song
of the s-AI-rens and go crazy
because rationality
is simply accepting a ration,
a bite of salt
to fight off idiocy.
Call an ambulance
nino-nino.

Lying down, speaking skies

like wet clothes

of a starry lake.

The flood

It wants to throw you to the ground

and into the mud

to feel well the boundaries to break

until you shine in the darkness

of a desperate river.

Sing Siren Sing

Eyes of children
waiting on the cliffs
sailors of flesh
wounded scream for help
hidden in the darkness
voices of serpents touch
the other side of the sea.

Pushing a Boy

Kurt Cobain

didn't commit suicide,

he was killed by the record labels.

Pushing a boy

with serious stomach

and chronic anxiety problems

into continuous

and exhausting tours

just for money,

when he needed

rest and detoxification.

Pushing a boy

to release all his hits

on one album, when

he could have ensured

a career of at least a decade:
all the tracks of Nevermind
are potential singles.

Pushing a boy
to feel worthless
and to shoot himself with a rifle in a field
while on the turntable
the vinyl of
"Automatic for the People" by REM
played its last track.

What's more automatic than death?

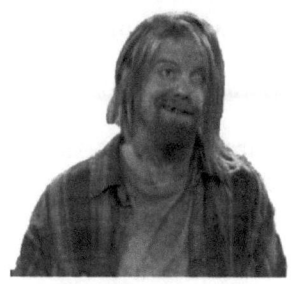

The last photo of Kurt Cobain R.I.P. (1994)

***

She posts it

In the empty corridors,

a woman walks at night

with a blade,

I mean a knife.

Always this woman

who walked through the corridors at night

at a certain point

suddenly,

senselessly

tears and cuts
people who had been
previously tied to their beds
and probably 90% drugged.
Then, with red blood
on white sheets,
she writes good morning.
She pulls out her iPhone 18 and takes a photo
applies the "hotness" filter
and posts it.

***

Moray eels

She strokes arms

scratched by cats

alone she walks on black cliffs

to Sampieri.

Frank Sinatra

He was a shitty guy

son of the neighborhood mafia boss

already as a kid

he roamed in gangs threatening

and having people beaten up.

He never stopped,

he didn't hesitate to have journalists beaten,

threatened, abused, corrupted.

His concertsnwere the perfect opportunity

to bring together

mafiosi and politicians

without too much embarrassment.

Did you know that it was actually him

who threw poor Marilyn

into Kennedy's bed?

He was a mobster.

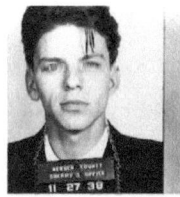 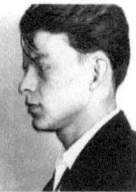

But what a voice!

Copy/Paste

Birds don't sing

but they scream.

Please keep it clean,

because the hand that cleans

is the same one you need for a drink.

Thank you!

The Staff

Slow worms

move

among forgotten objects.

Beyond a fence

a woman collects

glass and wraps it

in a cloth.

In the sea floats

the dead body

of a fisherman.

In a previous life

I was naked on the street

covered in whipped cream

and the two girls

who played the prank on me

didn't even give it to me.

BONUS

Did you know that "desiderio" (desire)

means to stay under the stars

(De-sidero)

and anxiously wait

to see your comrades return alive

from battle?

You can use this one

when you're with a wom*n

you like under a starry sky

and the make-out session is guaranteed.

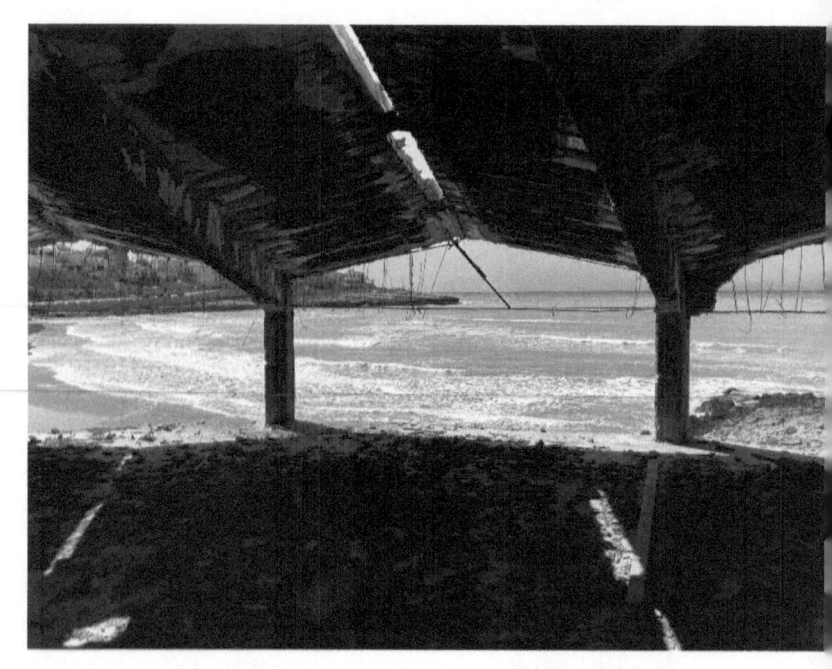

The Sea

Outside of society

but there is the sea.

The young sailor

Brooding by the window

he watches the harbor

he sinks his body and

drags with him

the words of the sea

in the light of dawn

maybe a bit of exercise

would do him good

like a team sport.

The sea is

an AM radio station

interference of white noise

and foam that

masks thoughts

birthing on the sand

labyrinths of poetry

(with seashells).

But the surfers

when the sea

is really

messy

where the hell are they?

Diary falling into the sea

wandering soul and footsteps

scraping with nails

the skin of the sun

while masked faces

melt away

in the empty night.

The dream of a summer
that comes and goes
I wait for the storm
there's a crab looking at me
but then he doesn't give a fuck.

Grey skies

stretches of wet sand

the walls of houses

marked by time

empty bodies walking

at the edge of the cliff

the distant sound of the sea

is the word of ghosts.

The flesh tears

the net of words

like a shark

and swiftly slips away

through the sea and through orgasms

chewed by time.

Crab

Behind a slab of butter

the heart breaks endlessly

on a plate for you

my crab meat.

Children play

in the morning

they inhale the sky

black and blow it

onto the sails of boats

but don't they go to school?

Aleph

I dissolve the corpse

the bond of truth

I wander, I set sail, I navigate

I become sail and wind

I dance face to face

towards the belly

of life

hooray

alive

w

v

Ink shoulder bumps in the air
to shake off the world's cords
but thought is a color to lie down
and the world is a wave already asleep.

Sicily

Violent sun

that with rays

presses up to the stars

that screams and burns.

Yet outside

everything is so dim,

the people, the fields, the sea.

No one seems to notice the horror.

Frankly**

No pretext

carousel of colors!

I change skin -

I cut.

My sea

Infinite;

as if it were waiting...

I get lost in it.

The paths of your hands:

golden flower.

Your eyes.

Melancholy weighs heavy!

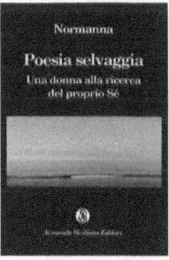

* Randomly selected verse mash-up from the beautiful book 'Poesia selvaggia' by Normanna, which I recommend you buy!

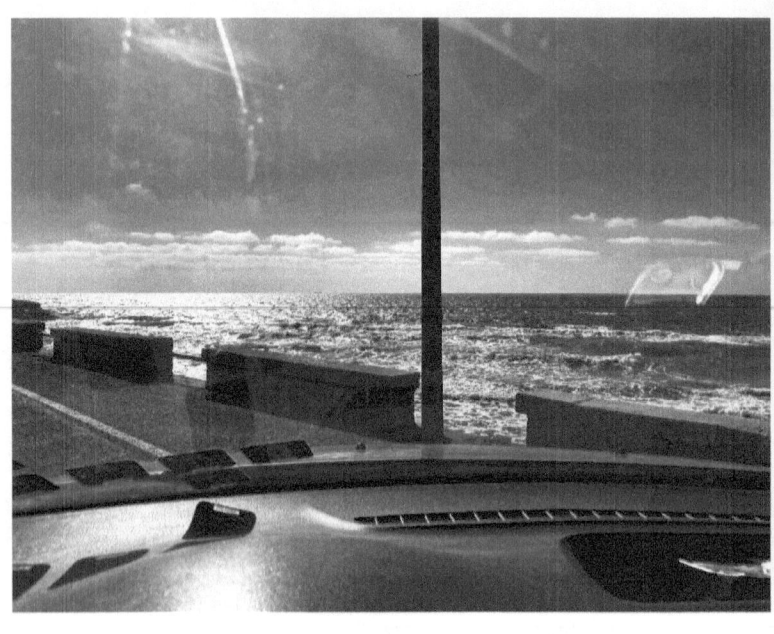

THE VOID

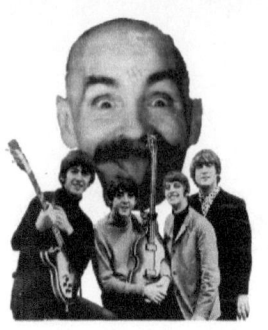

The most beautiful album

in the history of pop

is "Pet Sounds" by the Beach Boys

and this the Beatles

and Charles Manson

knew very well.

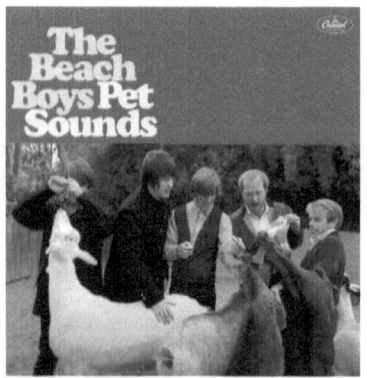

Italian madness,

imperfection like a postcard,

let's have coffee.

I feel the pain

in this two-bit guitar

out of tune and sweaty

I shoot the deer in the head

and I run away

shot and goal

fake applause.

I scream

Yesterday apocalypse
of water with ice cream.

People screaming and running.

The ice cream man
stops
making ice cream.

***

The greatness of artists

We were playing at a mountain resort
or rather, we were providing background music,
among the guests Lelex and Ferretti
who didn't even pretend
to listen for half a minute.

From the Ferrettis, not a clap, not a greeting,
not a nod, not even out of courtesy
for the less fortunate colleagues
at the bottom of the show business food chain.

Two days later
we were playing at a hotel in Milan
(still as background music)
and who sits in front of us

in the empty garden?

Mick Jagger of the Rolling Stones who,

sipping a couple of glasses of red,

listens to us for the entire set (45min)

then thanks us, shakes our hands,

we talk for a few minutes

and in the end, he leaves us

a gigantic tip.

***

Never underestimate

the importance of the sock.

Bet

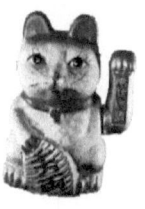

I went to buy a cat

because it wants to scare the mouse,

I went to buy the ruler

because I want to measure it,

I went to buy a Rolex

because I'm not a bum,

I went to play poker

but I lost the cat, the lizard, and the Rolex.

I went to buy a GameBoy

because I wanna play Super Mario,

I went to buy the car

because I want to park it,

I went to buy a dragon

because I'm tired of the cat,

I went to play poker

but I lost the GameBoy, the car, and the dragon.

My mind is a sand serpent

slipping through my fingers

but who cares?

People want to laugh.

Made In Italy

Elderly with iPhones

toasting

to Italian excellence

(because anything done in Italy

is automatically excellent)

meanwhile

somewhere in Pakistan

a pimply seventeen-year-old

in his basement

with his laptop

is already fucking us

in the ass.

Dead space

Stereo transfers +

Lost starry roads +

A burnt lynx +

Parades of secrets +

Fiery chambers +

Cancelling laments +

New liquid +

Naked eyes +

Fleeing dogs +

Exotic promises =
_____

a dangerous method.

The body is dragged

by an endless dark current.

The spirit clings

to a secret

a false memory

to avoid drowning.

It still tasted like a dream

looks at the phone

no one is looking for him

no one finds him

he goes back to bed.

In the morning,

he unfolds his thoughts and

wants them laid out

close to silence.

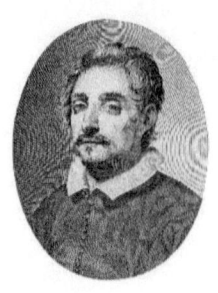

In my work

as a music composer

(still for a little while),

my greatest inspiration

is undoubtedly the great

Girolamo Frescobaldi.

Not for any of his historical or artistic merits,

but precisely because of his name...

If someone named like that made it,

there's hope for everyone.

Poor creatures

strictly impersonal

trash-endentes

talking about the sea

and other crap

buying toilet paper

and detergent.

No one at dawn

Dogs fight

behind a house

and they bite each other.

A friend

who hadn't had sex

for several months

went

to a Colombian prostitute

and liked it.

Game of love

Ball of fire in my hands

who will I throw it to tomorrow?

Doctor with the scalpel please

take my heart away.

Stung by the tarantula of poetry
I proclaim myself a poet
symptom of Italian mediocrity
arrogant in provincial solitude.

I enjoy the last
gleams of computer
before the AI-pocalypse.

In the corners the spiders
brighten up the house
and keep me company.

Nothing to write
just a stroll on the beach.

What will you have?
Cappuccino, coffee
and a croissant if there's one.

***

Hypnosatanic Millenials

We are damaged goods

or rather, spoiled crap

broken machines

that wheeze

and don't start.

We yearn

for the winning formula

following shadows of erased footprints.

We haven't understood anything.

So we curl up

in a fetal position

inside that gap

between wakefulness and sleep.

Please,

let's reclaim the idea of the future

we had in the past.

***

Λάθε Βιώσας

Live on the side

like the ancient Egyptians

not "in the face"

like Africans.

Live on Instagram

like the presumed ass-IAs of influencers

not Facebook

which is old people stuff.

Live in profile

live expanded

get high just right

choose life.

***

The last beach

Bloody feet

on the shimmering glass sand.

Yin and Yang

alternate

in a labyrinthine

and agonizing routine like

the sound of a deck of cards

shuffling endlessly.

One step at a time,

I take off my shoes.

Binary brain

black pen scribbling

on the same circle

like a black whirlpool

on your white swan

neck.

Funny humanity,

dancing a bit of coolness,

a few pieces for the employees

on red or black

but it's zero.

Everything goes up in flames,

all human constructions

all of nature.

Head trauma

to the barefoot rider

from the wild horse.

Fire spares only

those who walk

underneath the soles.

Blood highway

on the shimmering glass sand.

***

Eurovision 2024

Three hours left

I bet all the money I had

even the money for groceries

on Baby Lasagna (Croatia),

damn if he doesn't win

how much the hell did

this poem cost me?

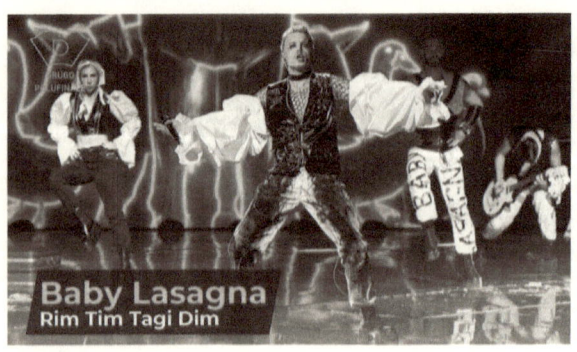

Dithering*

Weril uwbg veriufh bvkihu

aew ògo i q3gh4p9tp 394g8h

trnjg ge on erno

rrn eròoi 43fh3489qp hybel

q3drtnp dht 8o934o nq3

qzd sb3filuh o ne c2pq cnhf

ml ykiuy4pm qjp34 m pjqc

wer gffo frojm gwqipfm

ermxp 29cnoef3uhv nrog mp

uyh tgf gg cmpwe rigpow erwp.

* Google it!

A book, a song, a painting
are infinite. You just need to choose
when to end them.

THE END

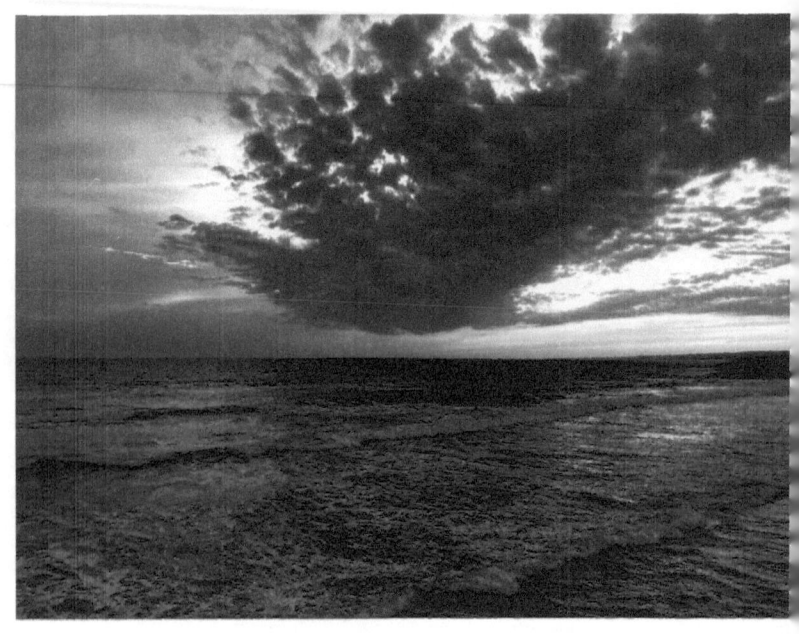

FOREWORD TO THE ENGLISH EDITION

by Gloria Occhipinti

"Until eighteen, everyone writes poetry; after, only two categories of people can continue to do so: poets and idiots." B. Croce

Could I not think of Benedetto Croce when it comes to poetry over 18? I could, but I can't, and so I approach Claudio's versification with the same distrust that we normally reserve for the insights of the son of two cousins. And I discover that we should welcome everything with a preconceived arrogance, ready to crumble, cracking in front of the unexpected, the unforeseen, the surprise, punishing us with enchantment.

A surprise is a surprise just as a rose is a rose as certain women would say (thanks Claudio) and certain men of the web.

If the unconscious still has something to tell us, it is often the recklessness that reserves us the best words.

I would really reserve a tight and prolonged embrace for Claudio's recklessness, for the unabashed, arrogant, reckless delicacy that has unconsciously translated him from the prosaic to the lyrical, from the physical to the metaphysical.

I immediately fall into the trap of references but they are only personal expedients and refuges, and I discover in Claudio's metaphysical, dreamlike shots, a Lynchian filter: as if David Lynch were intermittently possessed by Dario Vergassola and Mago Forrest, and dilated the banality of everyday life by diving into it with enchantment and dismay (thanks Claudio).

Fixed shots of Suns burning with paper inside that have become silver snakes, prostitutes who are statues of steam, and then Tano, the husband of the daughter of the lady from the tobacconist's who interrupts the archaic mythological metaphysics.

A mini-interior cinema, sometimes specialized in a tenderly childlike porn, or in the projection of fixed shots where beauty is corroded by pixels and thunder takes the form of a diamond, where out-of-place and out-of-time dialectical formulas burst forth, cleansed of the folkloric ridicule that Montalbano or whoever had sadly accustomed us to.

It's as if Claudio had finally awakened the unconscious, waking it from the little bed we relegated it to, and it had risen and walked and taken us by the hand, leading us to dance. Claudio drags us into this dance of the World to surf or float lightly, to soar in a suspended atmosphere dense with emotional steam, which becomes a cloud sometimes, but which falls back on us refreshing us, through those corridors, those openings where the purest folly bursts forth and the ironic discards the mask of intelligence, returning to be pure tickling.

This is Claudio's poetry: a mother blowing on her child's eyes giving him a euphoric moment of dreamy apnea in the intimacy of a diaper change.

Gloria Occhipinti

PROMOTIONAL MESSAGE

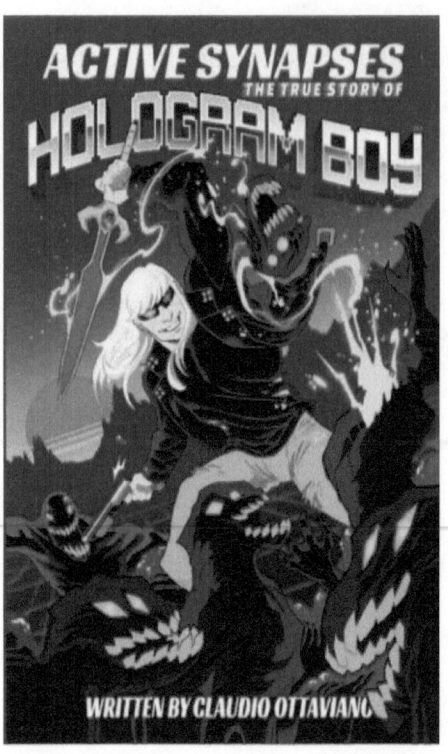

Discover the sensational story of Claudio, a sleazy jazz musician who, during lockdown, explores virtual reality and becomes Hologram Boy™.

"**Active Synapses**" is an exciting, fun, and unconventional book that, with its hilarious humor, invites you to get lost and discover new unexpected horizons.

BUY NOW ON AMAZON

CREDITS

Reader: You

Preface: Andrea G.G. Parasiliti

Foreword: Gloria Occhipinti

Art director: Lorenzo Ottaviano (my cousin)

Cover photo: Marco Cappello

Other photos: iPhone

Quality control: Mr. Nobody

All non-original images contained in this book are used for fair use under Article 70 of the Italian Copyright Law (L.633/1941).

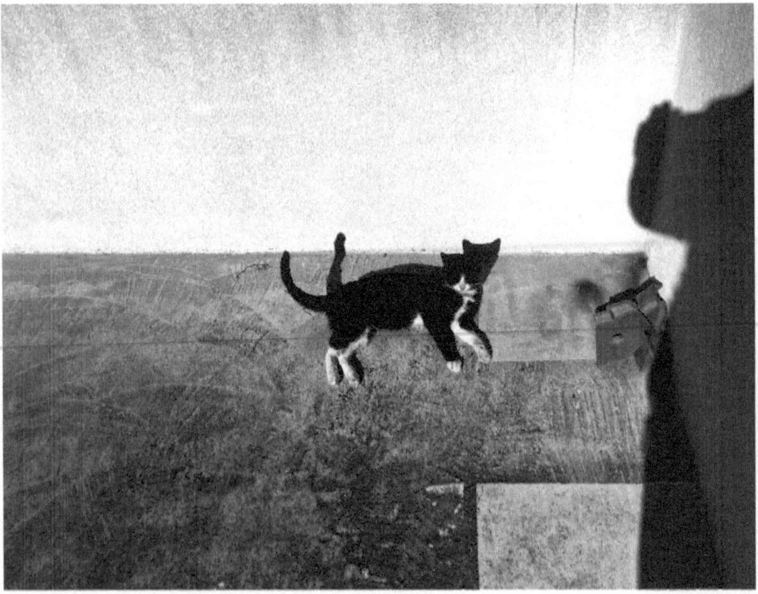

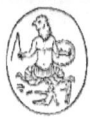

TABLE OF CONTENTS

PREFACE by Andrea G.G. Parasiliti………. pag.7

EXOCULATIONS……………………...…… pag.11

HORIZON ……………………................ pag.35

NOCTURNAL ANIMALS ………………. pag.57

THE SIRENS ……………………….....… pag.85

THE SEA …………………………………… pag.107

THE VOID …………………………..…… pag.123

FOREWORD by Gloria Occhipinti…..…… pag.153

PROMOTIONAL MESSAGE…………….pag.156

CREDITS ………………………………….. pag.157

TABLE OF CONTENTS ………………. pag.159

WWW.CLAUDIOOTTAVIANO.COM

www.ingramcontent.com/pod-product-compliance
Lightning Source LLC
Chambersburg PA
CBHW020423220526
45464CB00002B/547